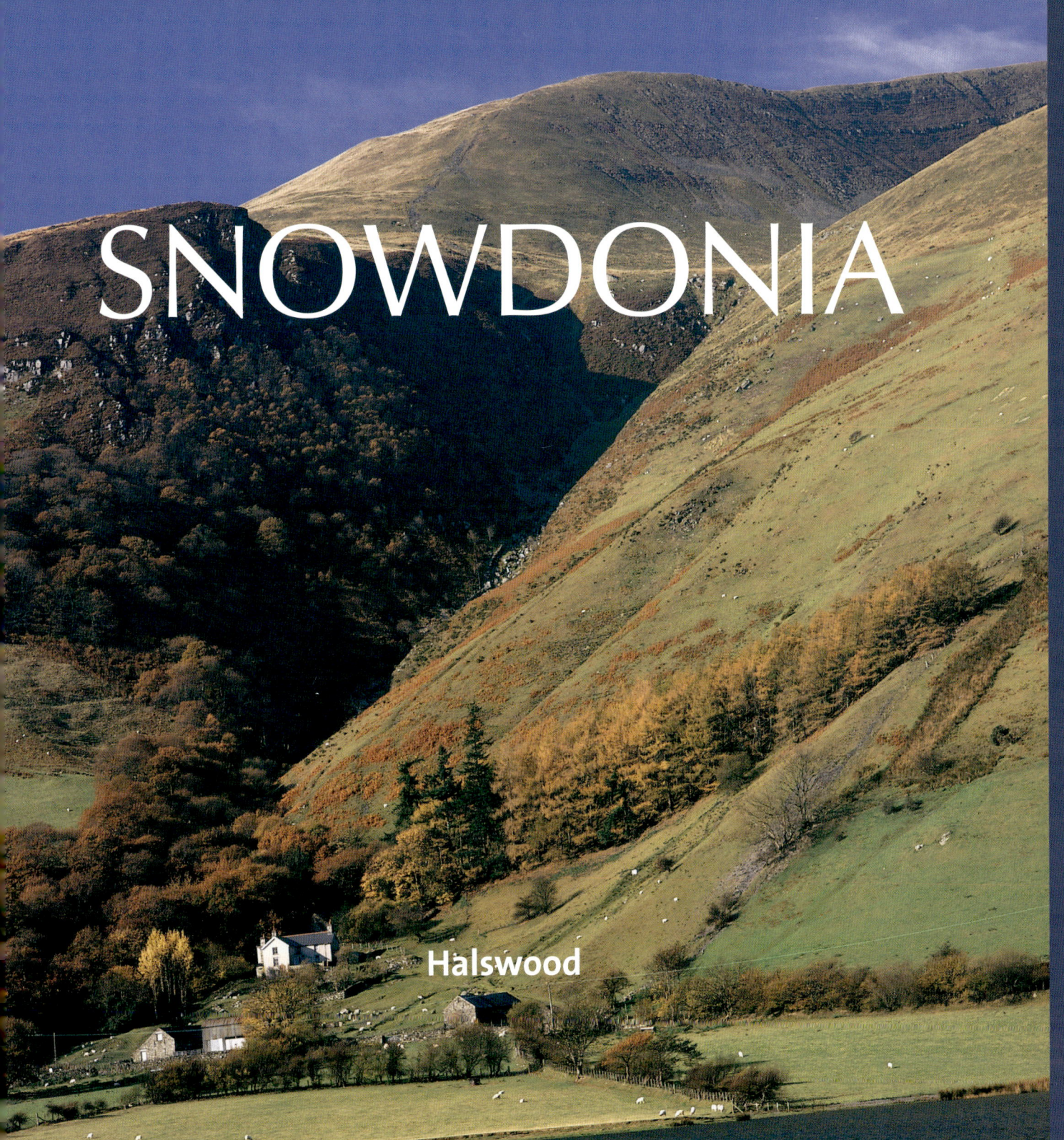

SNOWDONIA

Halswood

ADDRESS BOOK

Published by Halswood Stationers

Copyright © Halswood Stationers
Image copyright © The Estate of Jerry Rawson

All rights reserved. No part of this publication may be reproduced, stored in a retrieval system, or transmitted in any form or by any means without the prior permission of the copyright holder.

British Library Cataloguing-in-Publication Data
A CIP record for this title is available from the British Library

ISBN 978 0 85717 007 1

HALSWOOD STATIONERS
Halsgrove House,
Ryelands Industrial Estate,
Bagley Road, Wellington, Somerset TA21 9PZ
Tel: 01823 653777   Fax: 01823 216796
email: sales@halsgrove.com

Part of the Halsgrove group of companies
Information on all Halsgrove titles is available at:
www.halsgrove.com

Printed and bound in China by
Toppan Leefung Printing Ltd (0)

Front cover: The Snowdon hills in their winter blanket reflected in Llynnau Mymbyr, near Capel Curig.

Back cover: The setting sun highlights the flanks of Cadair Idris at the head of the Dysynni Valley.

Title page: An isolated farm at the foot of Cwm Amarch overlooking Llyn Mwyngil at Tal y Llyn.

Overleaf: The sand dunes at Harlech lead the eye towards Porthmadog, backed by the shapely peak of Moel Hebog.

The cascades of Rhaeadr-fawr – usually known as Aber Falls – on the northern slopes of the Carneddau near Abergwyngregyn.

INTRODUCTION

The Snowdonia National Park – *Parc Cenedlaethol Eryri* in Welsh – was designated as a National Park in 1951, and lies in the north-west corner of Wales. It contains some of the most spectacular and tightly packed mountain scenery in the United Kingdom.

It is a land of heather moors, lakes, wooded valleys, rivers, waterfalls and brooding, craggy mountain ranges. Within the boundary of the 827 square miles (2142 sq km) of the national park there are 23 miles (37 km) of coastline with beaches, sand dunes, and great sweeping bays, such as Tremadog and Mawddach. This means that it is difficult to escape the sea, and from many mountain tops you can catch glimpses of it.

Snowdonia offers great opportunities to landscape photographers and each season has its own beauty, from the colourful display of wild flowers in the valleys during springtime; the purple-clad heather moors above in high summer; the golden autumnal colours of ancient woods; to the vast Arctic-like winter plateau of the Carneddau, the rugged Glyderau and especially majestic Snowdon (Yr Wyddfa), at 1085m/3560 feet, the highest summit in England and Wales. All these bristling summits look especially spectacular when cloaked in snow.

Chasing the light across this precious landscape can be very rewarding, but it also poses a considerable challenge. You can be sitting on the top of a hill waiting for the sun to rise, only to find a bank of cloud rolling in from the east blocking out the magical dawn light. Or sheltering behind rocks waiting for heavy rain to pass over and leave storm clouds and dramatic light. The best photographic conditions are often around dawn and dusk, when the light can be a revelation, transforming a mundane landscape into something quite sublime. Patience to simply sit and wait for the ideal moment is essential – and that is what master photographer Jerry Rawson demonstrates again and again in the collection of superb images reproduced here.

Address books tend to be well used and have a long life. Along with important contact details, they keep track of the user's friends and acquaintances, tracing their lives over time and from place to place. And, if properly attended to, an address book eventually becomes a journal in itself, and an attractive and permanent keepsake. Whether bought as a gift or for personal use, this *Snowdonia Address Book*, with its superb pictorial reminders of the national park, will provide years of pleasure.

USEFUL ADDRESSES AND TELEPHONE NUMBERS

A

The sun sets over the Snowdon hills.

A

The first light of a cold winter's dawn adds
a rosy-pink hue to the Snowdon hills.

B

An early morning view of Y Garn and Foel-goch reflected in the calm waters of Llyn Ogwen.

B

B

B

Gylder Fach reflected in Llyn y Caseg-fraith

C

Vibrant purple heather adds colour to this summer scene of a stream rushing down the slopes from Llyn Idwal.

C

C

C

The sun sets beyond the Snowdon hills in this view across Llynnau Mymbyr, near Capel Curig.

D

The rounded, grassy Moel Eilio, which overlooks Llanberis, is seen in this view across Cwm Dwythwch, from the slopes of Moel Cynghorion.

D

D

D

A solitary tree acts as a focal point in this winter view across Nant Gwynant to Crib Goch.

E

Croesor, a village forever associated with the slate industry, which has formed such an integral part of the history and heritage of this region. The hill in the background is Moel Hebog.

E

E

E

The rocks at the top of Y Gribin, a ridge on Glyder Fach, lead the eye across Llyn Idwal to Y Garn backed by Foel-goch, with the trench of Nant Ffrancon, a classic glacial trough, on the right.

F

Misty morning on Llyn Tegid looking south to Aran Benllyn.

F

F

F

Erosion by wind and rain has created this remarkable cluster of rocks on the summit slopes of Glyder Fawr. Y Garn in the background.

G

Early morning light illuminates this eastern view from the north ridge of Aran Benllyn to the distant hills of Moel Llyfnant and Arenig Fawr.

G

G

G

Looking east from Aran Fawddwy to the distant rolling hills of the Berwyn.

H

The Afon Glaslyn tumbles down the hillside below the mist-shrouded Cwm Dyli on the eastern flanks of Snowdon (Yr Wyddfa).

H

H

H

The imposing Rhinog Fawr and Rhinog Fach on the skyline seen from the road to Maes-y-garnedd at the head of Cwm Nantcol.

The superb sandy beach at Harlech.

Slate fences line up like tombstones at the disused Rhosydd slate quarry, on the high pass between Blaenau Ffestiniog and Croeser.

J

A house shrouded in red foliage on the
shore of Llyn Mwyngil at Tal y Llyn

J

Two types of heather, ling and bell, and the golden flowers of gorse create a colourful foreground of this view above Llyn Cregennen near Arthog, with the Cadair Idris range in the background.

K

The Afon Clywedog, to the east of Dolgellau, rushes between glistening rocks and gullies. The water is frozen in motion, creating a silky veil.

K

A fiery sunset reflected in the waters of
the Afon Mawddach, near Bontddu.

L

The aptly named Craig yr Aderyn (Bird Rock) in the Dysynni Valley, is the haunt of many species of birds including cormorants, which are normally coastal dwellers.

L

The ruins of Castell y Bere, situated on a rocky mound, in its secluded location at the head of the Dysynni Valley with the Cadair Idris range rising behind it.

M

The afterglow of the setting sun has created a moody atmosphere in this shot of the sea and boulders near Llanbedr, with the Lleyn Peninsula on the distant horizon.

M

M

M

The summit slopes of Y Garn reflected in Llyn y Cwn, a small lake situated in a hollow overlooking the Devil's Kitchen in Cwm Idwal.

N

A summer's evening by Llyn Padarn near Llanberis, with the Snowdon range mirrored in the calm water.

N

The Snowdon hills in their winter blanket reflected in Llynnau Mymbyr, near Capel Curig. A classic view of Snowdon.

O

o

Veils of mist swirl around the summits of Snowdon (Yr Wyddfa) and Crib Goch, which in conditions like these look almost like Himalayan giants.

O

The last rays of evening sunshine catch the summit slopes of Moel Hebog in this view across Llyn Gwynant.

PQ

Low evening sunlight casts long shadows across the hillside near Llangynog, the Berwyn hills.

PQ

PQ

The trees enliven this view across the slopes of Craig Llwyd overlooking Minffordd.

R

An evening view east across the Mawddach Estuary to the Cadair Idris range seen from the rugged hillside of Dinas Oleu, above Barmouth.

R

An autumn view up to the head of the Valley of the Afon Dysynni (the Dysynni Valley) to the north-east of Towyn.

S

A lone boulder acts as a foreground in this view across to the Lleyn Peninsula, from the beach at Llandanwg.

S

The setting sun highlights the flanks of Cadair Idris at the head of the Dysynni Valley.

T

Evening light on the northern section of the Cadair Idris range reflected in Llyn Cregennen.

T

T

An autumn view of Craig Maesglase, which is part of the gentle Dyfi hills situated to the east of Dinas Mawddwy.

UV

The last rays of the setting sun light up the mouth of the Mawddach Estuary, and the sand spit of Ro Wen, at Barmouth

UV

Storm clouds sweep over Moel Sych and, on the right, the pointed hill of Cadair Berwyn.

W

The outflow from Llyn Ogwen backed by Tryfan.

W

The soft play of evening light picks out the west-facing cliffs of Cadair Idris, in this view across the Afon Mawddach.

XYZ

The last rays of the setting sun touch boulders and add warmth to this view north across Tremadog Bay, from the beach near Llandanwg.

XYZ